IMAGES
of America

TENNESSEE'S UNION
CAVALRYMEN

The Tennessee state capitol in Nashville, completed in 1859, became the center of the secession debate and the headquarters of military governor Andrew Johnson. (LOC.)

IMAGES
of America

TENNESSEE'S UNION
CAVALRYMEN

Myers E. Brown II with the
Tennessee State Museum

ARCADIA
PUBLISHING

Published by Arcadia Publishing
Charleston SC, Chicago IL, Portsmouth NH, San Francisco CA

Printed in the United States of America

Library of Congress Catalog Card Number: 2008929806

For all general information contact Arcadia Publishing at:
Telephone 843-853-2070
Fax 843-853-0044
E-mail sales@arcadiapublishing.com
For customer service and orders:
Toll-Free 1-888-313-2665

Visit us on the Internet at www.arcadiapublishing.com

To Tennessee's Unionists:
may their loyalty and their actions,
both good and bad, not be forgotten.

CONTENTS

ACKNOWLEDGMENTS

Many people assisted with this volume. First and foremost, my supervisors and coworkers at the Tennessee State Museum provided endless amounts of support for this project, and many of the images featured in the book reside in the museum's extensive Civil War collection. The following institutions and individuals provided assistance in locating and acquiring copies of the images: Dr. Arthur Bergeron and the staff of the U.S. Army Military History Institute; Sally Polhemus, archivist, the McClung Historical Collection of the Knoxville Public Library at the East Tennessee Historical Society; Annette Hartigan, librarian, Great Smoky Mountains National Park; Michelle McDonald, curator, East Tennessee History Center; and the great staff of the Tennessee State Library and Archives. All of the above named institutions were extremely efficient and delivered the images in record time.

I would be remiss if I failed to mention the excellent digital collection available online through the Library of Congress. We are blessed to have these collections available at no cost. Several individuals also contributed photographs, information, research, or assistance on the project, including Dr. Doug Locke, Scott W. Gilmer, David Jarnagin, Bob White, Mick Morin, Brad Kavan, and Amber Barfield. The Tennessee Civil War National Heritage Area provided funding for the Tennessee State Museum's traveling exhibition, Hoofbeats in the Heartland: Civil War Cavalry in Tennessee. As curator of this exhibition, I realized the quantity and quality of images of Tennessee's loyal troopers, which inspired me to pursue this project. Maggie Bullwinkel, my editor with Arcadia Publishing, has been extremely patient, understanding, and a joy with which to work.

Lastly, I would like to thank my family, especially my wife, Angie, and my daughter, Morgan, for tolerating my late nights, short temper, and neglect of household chores while I worked on this project. Angie also assisted me with editing and research, and remains my closest friend and confidant. She is the love of my life and constantly reminds me to "Be joyful always, pray continually, and give thanks in all circumstances, for this is God's will for you in Christ Jesus" (I Thessalonians 5:16–18).

—Myers Brown
July 2008

INTRODUCTION

The secession crisis of 1860–1861 found Tennesseans split over the question. Initially, Tennessee voters rejected the notion of leaving the Union and joining the Confederacy. The attack on Fort Sumter changed many things. Indeed, a peaceful resolution between North and South now appeared impossible. Furthermore, U.S. president Abraham Lincoln called upon all loyal states to provide troops to put down the rebellion. Tennessee's governor refused to send troops against fellow Southerners, and soon the state seceded and joined the Confederacy. However, preservation of the Union remained strong among many Tennesseans, and the state provided more than 32,000 white troops to the Union cause.

Although pockets of Unionist sentiment could be found in every grand division of the state, the majority of loyal Tennesseans were concentrated in the counties of East Tennessee. In general terms, as one gradually moved from East Tennessee into Middle Tennessee and on to West Tennessee, the Unionist sentiment waned. Not surprisingly, the pro-Union sentiment corresponded proportionally to the number of slaves in each grand division. West and Middle Tennessee relied heavily on cash crops such as tobacco and cotton, both of which required slave labor. Meanwhile, East Tennessee's mountainous terrain, pocked with small valleys, encouraged more subsistence farming and thus required less slave labor. Although the majority of Unionists remained in the east, each grand division ultimately provided men to the Union cavalry. Tennessee's secession brought chaos, fear, and violence to the state's most outspoken Unionists. Some initially met in Greeneville and filed a petition to allow East Tennessee to secede from the rest of the state. The state legislature refused to vote on the petition. The East Tennessee and Virginia Railroad provided the most direct link between Richmond and the Deep South and was vitally important to the Confederacy. This rail line became an early target for opposition to the Confederacy, and many Union men attempted to burn the numerous bridges and trestles throughout East Tennessee.

The bridge burners brought the ire of the Confederate authorities down upon all Unionists, and reprisals soon followed. Forced to flee their homes, Union men began to form Tennessee regiments in the relative safety of neutral Kentucky. Thousands would leave homes, families, livelihoods, and fortunes to travel along mountain paths, through all types of weather, often pursued by Confederate home guards, to Cumberland Gap or other locales behind Union lines. Some Union men remained at home and began to form guerrilla bands to oppose Confederate authority, or they simply hid to avoid conscription.

Inspiring these men and women were their vocal political leaders, such as Andrew Johnson, Tennessee's senator and former governor; William Gannaway "Parson" Brownlow; Horace Maynard, a U.S. Congressman; William Bowen Campbell, another former governor; and military men such as David Glasgow Farragut and Samuel P. Carter. These men defiantly opposed secession and the Confederacy and often found their lives in danger.

In 1862, Nashville, Memphis, and much of Middle and West Tennessee fell to Union armies, and President Lincoln commissioned Andrew Johnson as brigadier general and military governor of the state. Johnson's appointment inspired Tennessee's Union population even further, but ironically, East Tennessee remained in Confederate hands until late 1863.

Union men in Middle and West Tennessee made their way to Union lines and enlisted, while the state spiraled into a violent form of guerrilla warfare. Keeping the guerrillas and the Confederate cavalry under control became a major priority for the Johnson administration. Johnson realized that large amounts of cavalry would be needed to deal with the raids launched by the Confederate cavalry commanded by Joe Wheeler, Nathan Bedford Forrest, and John Hunt Morgan, as well as the guerrillas, partisans, and bushwhackers, which seemed to be active in every county. Secretary of War Edwin Stanton authorized Johnson "to raise any amount of cavalry in your State that may be required for the service." Governor Johnson took this authorization to heart, and many Tennessee cavalry regiments were formed. Furthermore, Johnson managed to convert some former infantry regiments to cavalry and even mounted infantry units not officially re-designated as cavalry regiments. By war's end, Tennessee provided almost 14 regiments of cavalry (the 14th Tennessee was decimated at Fort Pillow and never reached full strength) and eight regiments of mounted infantry, and at least three of its infantry regiments spent part of their service on horseback. Tennessee raised no regiments of black troops that served mounted. Ironically, nearly all of Tennessee's Unionist cavalrymen and mounted infantrymen spent at least some of their service operating in their home state and often even in their home counties.

While over half of Tennessee's white Union regiments served in some capacity as mounted troops, the quality varied from unit to unit. Some units were of excellent quality, such as the 1st Tennessee Cavalry, commanded first by Col. Robert Johnson and later by Col. James Brownlow. The unit served throughout the Western theater and provided the state with its only Civil War Medal of Honor winner. Others were noted for ill discipline, poor leadership, or worse, and in some instances, they were little better than the guerrillas against which they operated.

Superiors often complained about the Tennesseans. Gen. William T. Sherman wrote of Gen. Alvan Gillem's Tennessee Brigade, "I have always regarded General Gillem's command as a refuge hospital for indolent Tennesseans." Meanwhile Gen. Richard Johnson complained, "[I have] several regiments of Tennessee cavalry claiming to be independent of General Sherman or any one else save Andy Johnson. These regiments violate safeguards, rob, and murder in open daylight and refuse to report the facts to any one except the Governor." Gen. James Wilson, overall commander of the cavalry in the military district of Mississippi, stated in regards to Tennessee cavalry regiments, "With the exception of the First Tennessee they are all worthless." Nevertheless, Gen. Edward McCook noted after the war, "God bless your old East Tennessee souls, don't you know your loyalty and devotion gave us of the North courage to fight, when everything looked like the darkness of despair? I had two Southern Brigades, one of Tennessee and one from Kentucky. I can't say that their discipline was perfect, but their fighting was."

With the end of the Civil War, Tennessee's Unionists controlled the state government, and many former troopers served in the State Guard during Reconstruction. With the return to power of Tennessee's former Confederates in the early 1870s, however, the service of Tennessee's Union troopers slipped from prominence, and the "Lost Cause" all but washed their service from the public consciousness. Regardless of the quality of their unit, these men risked their lives, their families, and their fortunes to fight for the Union cause. All of these loyal cavaliers suffered for the Union; many of them paid with their lives. This volume only begins to tell their story.

Throughout the text, the terms "loyal" and "Unionist" are used interchangeably, and, unless otherwise stated, referenced units are presumed to be both Union and cavalry regiments. I have also utilized abbreviations in the photograph credits. They are as follows: GSMNP (Great Smoky Mountains National Park), LOC (Library of Congress), TSLA (Tennessee State Library and Archives), TSM (Tennessee State Museum), MOLLUS (Military Order of the Loyal Legion of the United States), and USAMHI (U.S. Army Military History Institute).

—Myers Brown
July 2008

One

A Tailor, a Preacher, and Three Sea Captains

Foremost among those opposing secession, or Unionists as they became known, was Sen. Andrew Johnson. Johnson, a former tailor in Greeneville, served as governor before representing Tennessee in the U.S. Senate. Johnson refused to give up his Senate seat after Tennessee's secession, and he subsequently became the most recognized leader of the Unionist cause. Following Johnson's example, Rep. Horace Maynard, a Knoxville attorney, refused to leave his Congressional seat. Both men returned to Tennessee in an effort to restore the state to the Union but ultimately fled Confederate authorities.

Despite threats to his life, the destruction of his printing office, and an arrest by Confederate authorities, William Gannaway "Parson" Brownlow, a Methodist minister and newspaper editor, openly opposed the Confederates. After fleeing to Kentucky, Brownlow toured the North to win support for Tennessee Unionists. He set aside his old rivalry with Andrew Johnson to further the Union cause in Tennessee.

Samuel Powhatan Carter and David Glasgow Farragut were both East Tennesseans and career navy officers. Both men remained loyal to the Union and inspired others to remain true to the cause, while William Driver, a native of Massachusetts, had spent a lifetime at sea before moving to Nashville. He hid his American flag, "Old Glory," until Nashville fell to Union troops in February 1862.

Noteworthy Unionists in Middle Tennessee included William Bowen Campbell and William Brickle Stokes. Campbell, a Sumner County attorney, was a veteran of the Mexican War and served as the last Whig governor. He refused to join the Confederate cause and accepted a commission in the Union army. Stokes was a livestock farmer and politician in DeKalb County before the war. With guerrilla activity on the rise, Stokes fled to the Union army and raised his own command.

Regardless of their backgrounds, these men became the leaders of the Unionist cause in Tennessee. Interestingly, the Civil War unified many of these former political enemies behind the cause of preserving the Union, and they inspired thousands of men to join the army.

Andrew Johnson moved to Greeneville, Tennessee, in 1826, where he worked as a tailor, but he soon began a political career. He served as alderman, mayor, representative, congressman, and governor. The secession crisis found Johnson serving as a Democrat in the U.S. Senate, and he returned to Tennessee and formed a pro-Union alliance with former Whig rivals such as William Brownlow. When Tennessee seceded, Johnson refused to give up his seat in the Senate. (LOC.)

With the fall of Nashville in February 1862, President Lincoln, a Republican, appointed Johnson as military governor with the rank of brigadier general. Johnson struggled to control a state divided by loyalties, racked by guerrilla warfare, and devastated by campaigning armies. As military governor, he sought horses for many Tennessee units, including his son Robert Johnson's 1st Tennessee Cavalry. In 1864, Lincoln named Johnson as his vice presidential running mate. (LOC.)

As military governor, Johnson fortified the state capitol with entrenchments and gun emplacements. He feared an attack by pro-Confederate sympathizers in Nashville, as well as the possibility of a Confederate cavalry raid. This view shows Union siege guns covered for protection from the rain. (LOC.)

Within weeks of the Union army's arrival in Middle and West Tennessee, informal groups of pro-Confederate partisans began to harass the occupation forces. These partisans attacked rail lines, riverboats, small outposts, and isolated garrisons. Tennessee was plagued by guerrilla activities for the rest of the war. This May 1862 order from Governor Johnson was an attempt to curtail the activities by punishing the civilians who assisted them. (LOC.)

PROCLAMATION.

EXECUTIVE OFFICE,
Nashville, Tenn., May 9, 1862.

WHEREAS, Certain persons, unfriendly and hostile to the Government of the United States, have banded themselves together, and are now going at large through many of the counties in this State, arresting, maltreating and plundering Union citizens wherever found;

Now, therefore, I, ANDREW JOHNSON, Governor of the State of Tennessee, by virtue of the power and authority in me vested, do hereby proclaim that in every instance in which a Union man is arrested and maltreated by the marauding bands aforesaid, five or more rebels from the most prominent in the immediate neighborhood shall be arrested, imprisoned, and otherwise dealt with as the nature of the case may require; And further, in all cases in which the property of citizens loyal to the Government of the United States is taken or destroyed, full and ample remuneration shall be made to them out of the property of such rebels in the vicinity as have sympathized with, and given aid, comfort, information or encouragement to the parties committing such depredations.

This order will be executed in letter and spirit. All citizens are hereby warned under heavy penalties from entertaining, receiving or encouraging such persons so banded together or in any wise connected therewith.

By the Governor:
ANDREW JOHNSON.
EDWARD H. EAST,
Secretary of State.

Horace Maynard was a Massachusetts native but moved to Knoxville in 1838. After teaching at East Tennessee College, Maynard practiced law, was elected to Congress, and worked to prevent secession. He fled Knoxville after secession but, like Andrew Johnson, retained his Congressional seat. When Johnson became military governor, Maynard served as attorney general. He remained a stalwart example of devotion to the Union throughout the war. (TSM.)

After secession, Tennessee joined the Confederacy, and Unionists in East Tennessee planned to destroy bridges of the East Tennessee and Virginia Railroad, thus severing communications between Virginia and the Deep South. This woodcut from *Harper's Weekly* depicts loyal Tennesseans swearing an oath to the Union before initiating their plan to burn the bridges. (LOC.)

William Gannaway "Parson" Brownlow was a Whig newspaper editor and Methodist preacher in Knoxville before the war. After initially considering joining the secessionist cause, Brownlow became one of the most vocal opponents to Tennessee secession and was briefly arrested by Confederates in Knoxville. He fled to Kentucky and toured the Northern states to promote the plight of Unionists in Confederate-occupied Tennessee. (TSM.)

After the war, Brownlow served as Tennessee's Reconstruction governor and was noted for his hard-handed treatment of former Confederates and the Ku Klux Klan. Both of Brownlow's sons served in Union cavalry regiments. (LOC.)

Knoxville. April 22, 1861.

Gen Gideon J. Pillow,—I have just received your message, through Mr. Sale, requesting me to serve as Chaplain to your Brigade in the Southern Army; and in the spirit of kindness in which this request is made, but in all candor, I return for an answer, that when I shall have made up my mind to go to hell, I will cut my throat and go direct and not travel round by the way of the Southern Confederacy.—I am, very respectfully, &c.,

W. G. BROWNLOW.

Parson Brownlow.

William Gannaway "Parson" Brownlow briefly entertained the idea of joining the secessionists and the Provisional Army of Tennessee. Commander Gideon Pillow offered him a staff officer position. The envelope above bears his response in typical vitriolic Brownlow style: "If I am to go to hell I will not go by way of the Southern Confederacy." Strong statements such as this gave Unionists resolve to resist Confederate efforts. (TSM.)

Portland, May 31, 1862.

I am an unconditional Union men—for my God and Country, at all hazards and to the last extremity.

W. G. Brownlow

This note, dated May 31, 1862, from William Brownlow reads, "I am an unconditional Union man—for my God and Country, at all hazards and to the last extremity." Brownlow may have signed this note in Portland, Tennessee, or during his tour of the Northern states. (TSM.)

Union men in areas occupied by Confederate troops often suffered for their sentiments. Brownlow authored a short book to illustrate the plight of the Unionist in Confederate-occupied East Tennessee. The woodcut above, entitled "Murdering Union Men," is from Brownlow's book. (LOC.)

Samuel Powhatan Carter was one of five brothers from Elizabethton who supported the Union. Carter graduated from the U.S. Naval Academy in the class of 1846. A successful navy officer, Carter wrote an open letter of support for the Union in 1861, which caught the attention of President Lincoln. At the insistence of Lincoln, Carter reported to the army and commanded a cavalry raid into East Tennessee to attack the East Tennessee and Virginia Railroad. His raid was the first successful Union cavalry operation of the war. Carter remained with the army until the end of the war. After the war, he returned to the navy, where he obtained the rank of admiral. He is the only man in American history to hold both the rank of admiral and general. (TSM.)

David Glasgow Farragut was born near Knoxville in 1801 but joined the navy under the tutelage of his patron, Commodore David Porter, at age nine. He served in the War of 1812 at age 11 and made the navy his career. Farragut remained loyal to the Union with the coming of the Civil War. Farragut was the most successful navy officer of the conflict. He captured New Orleans, opened the Mississippi River up to Vicksburg, and essentially stopped Confederate shipping in the Gulf of Mexico by capturing Mobile Bay. In the later battle, with his attack stalled by a Confederate torpedo field, he supposedly exclaimed, "Damn the torpedoes! Full speed ahead." In 1866, as a reward for his successes and for his commitment to the Union, Farragut was named admiral of the U.S. Navy, the first American to hold such a title. (LOC.)

William Driver, a native of Massachusetts, relocated to Nashville in 1837 after 16 years at sea. During the Confederate occupation of Nashville, Driver sewed his American flag, which he dubbed "Old Glory," beneath a quilt. When Union troops arrived in February 1862, Driver produced "Old Glory," and it flew from the state capitol. The flag's nickname became popular, and his flag resides in the Smithsonian. Driver's actions inspired loyal Nashvillians, and he continued to support the Union throughout the war. (TSM.)

The most famous loyal Middle Tennessean was William Bowen Campbell. Campbell, an attorney, served with distinction in the Seminole and Mexican Wars and served as governor from 1851 to 1853. He openly opposed secession and received a commission as brigadier general in the Union army, but he soon resigned. After his resignation, Campbell worked tirelessly to have Tennessee restored to the Union and supported Andrew Johnson. In 1866, he represented Tennessee in Congress. (TSM.)

Bailey Peyton Sr. of Sumner County was a close friend and political ally of William Bowen Campbell and served in Congress prior to the war. This daguerreotype shows Colonel Peyton during the Mexican War. Like many Tennessee Whigs, Peyton Sr. remained a Union man during the Civil War. Meanwhile, his son Peyton Jr. served in the Confederate 20th Tennessee Infantry Regiment and died while fighting at Mill Springs, Kentucky, in January 1862. (TSM.)

John Bell was among the most prominent of Tennessee's politicians in the years just prior to the outbreak of the Civil War. Bell, a former Whig, was the Constitutional Union candidate for president in 1860 and actually won the popular vote in many Southern states. With the outbreak of war, Bell initially worked to keep Tennessee in the Union but reluctantly joined the Confederate cause, much to the disappointment of men like Peyton and Campbell. His decision ended his political career, and he lived in obscurity in Stewart County after the war. (LOC.)

William Brickle Stokes served in the Tennessee general assembly and as a U.S. congressman before the war and aligned himself with the Union in the fiercely divided area of the Cumberland Plateau of Middle Tennessee. When Confederate partisans and guerrillas swept through DeKalb County, Stokes joined Union forces near Murfreesboro and formed the 5th Tennessee Cavalry Regiment. He waged a brutal campaign against guerrillas and Confederate cavalry operating around his home county. Stokes and the guerrillas opposing him terrorized the region in a never-ending cycle of violence. Eventually, he took command of the Union garrison in Carthage, Tennessee, and conducted antiguerrilla operations, which often included depredations against civilians. Many considered Stokes little better than the guerrillas against which he operated. (LOC.)

Two

Loyal Leaders, the Military

While the loyal politicians inspired, influenced, and directed the Unionist cause, others became leaders along military lines, serving as generals, colonels, and other regimental officers. As more Unionists fled their homes to safe areas behind Union lines in Kentucky or Middle Tennessee, regiments were formed to fight against the Confederacy. In a time period where volunteer units elected their officers, political leaders, leading citizens, and members of influential families naturally transitioned into a military role. Some of these young men were the sons of leading Unionists, while those with natural leadership capabilities rose from relative obscurity to places of prominence and recognition. Some of these commanders were highly successful, while others struggled or failed miserably. Undoubtedly, these men were committed to the preservation of the Union. A soldier who joined the Union cause while his family remained in Confederate territory risked losing life, home, farm, or business. Furthermore, joining the Union army was normally no easy feat. Many traveled for hundreds of miles through rough terrain to reach friendly lines, while those in close proximity to safe areas risked ostracism and retribution from their pro-Confederate neighbors and guerrillas.

Initially, the Union cavalry operating in Tennessee was poorly organized, misunderstood by high-ranking officers such as Sherman and Grant, and often ineptly led on the brigade, division, and corps level. Only in 1864, under the leadership of James Harrison Wilson, was the Union cavalry consistently capable of competing with their Confederate counterparts. This chapter includes images of regimental officers who commanded Tennessee regiments, as well as images of higher-ranking officers under which the Tennessee regiments served. Company-grade officers, such as lieutenants and captains, are featured in the next chapter alongside the enlisted men they commanded.

Gen. Alvan Cullem Gillem was born in Gainesboro in Middle Tennessee and attended the U.S. Military Academy, graduating in the class of 1851. He remained loyal and commanded a brigade under George Thomas, a Union man from Virginia. He served as colonel of the 10th Tennessee Infantry and as provost marshal of Nashville before being appointed adjutant general of Tennessee by Andrew Johnson. Johnson favored Gillem over the navy officer Samuel Powhatan Carter because he believed the Carter brothers carried too much political influence. (LOC.)

In this image, General Gillem appears in his field uniform, which bears a simple star on the shoulder as opposed to the more formal shoulder boards. Many officers adopted this simplified, subdued insignia so that they were less conspicuous on the battlefield. In 1864, Gillem commanded the Governor's Guard, a brigade consisting of the 8th, 9th, 10th, and 13th Tennessee Cavalry Regiments, and led the expedition that surprised and killed Confederate general John Hunt Morgan in Greeneville. During the last months of the war and through Reconstruction, Gillem briefly served in the General Assembly and commanded several military districts. His close relationship with President Johnson resulted in his transfer to Texas after the election of 1868. (TSM.)

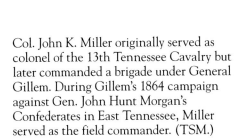

In this carte de visite from the photo album of Capt. Edgar Grisham of the 8th Tennessee, Gillem stands in his officer's frock coat with full insignia. Gillem autographed this carte de visite before presenting it to Captain Grisham. (TSM.)

Col. John K. Miller originally served as colonel of the 13th Tennessee Cavalry but later commanded a brigade under General Gillem. During Gillem's 1864 campaign against Gen. John Hunt Morgan's Confederates in East Tennessee, Miller served as the field commander. (TSM.)

Robert Johnson, the second oldest son of Andrew Johnson, fled East Tennessee after attempts to stop the secessionist movement failed. Working with other Tennessee Unionists, including the son of William Brownlow, Johnson formed the 4th Tennessee Infantry Regiment in Kentucky. After his father became military governor, the unit received horses and was renamed the 1st Tennessee Cavalry with Johnson as colonel and James Patton Brownlow as lieutenant colonel. Johnson's affiliation with the unit was short-lived. He was cashiered from the army in 1863 for alcoholism and died of a laudanum overdose in 1869. (MOLLUS Collection at USAMHI.)

James P. Brownlow (left) was the youngest son of William G. Brownlow and served as lieutenant colonel of the 1st Tennessee Cavalry. After Robert Johnson's resignation, Brownlow became colonel and commanded the regiment until late in the war. While fighting around Atlanta, Brownlow sent his command across the Chattahoochee River wearing nothing but hats and cartridge boxes. This naked attack so distracted the Confederates that Brownlow's men gained a foothold on the Southern side. James's older brother, John (below), served as lieutenant colonel of the 9th Tennessee Cavalry. John was expelled from Emory and Henry College because of a fight that resulted in the other student's death. The 9th Tennessee fought in numerous engagements late in the war as part of General Gillem's Governor's Guard. When his father became governor during Reconstruction, John took over as editor of the *Knoxville Whig*. (Left, MOLLUS Collection at USAMHI; below, TSM.)

Not all of Tennessee's Union leaders' sons joined cavalry regiments. Edward Maynard, the son of Horace Maynard, served as lieutenant colonel of the 6th Tennessee Infantry and commanded the regiment on campaigns throughout the Western Theater. The 6th was one of the few Tennessee infantry regiments that did not spend part of their service on horseback. (TSM.)

Andrew Johnson's sons-in-law also served the Union cause either as inspirational or as military leaders. Pictured here is David T. Patterson, who married Martha Johnson in 1855. A lawyer and judge, Patterson continued to serve as a circuit judge through most of the war. During Reconstruction, Patterson filled his father-in-law's seat in the Senate and cast a not-guilty vote during his impeachment trial. (LOC.)

Daniel Stover was married to Mary Johnson and was a farmer in Carter County. Upon Tennessee's secession, he attacked Confederate supply lines in East Tennessee and piloted Unionists to safety, including Mary and his mother-in-law, Eliza. He received a commission as colonel of the 4th Tennessee Infantry, but illness prevented him from actively commanding the unit. He died from disease in December 1864. (TSLA.)

Daniel Ellis, like Daniel Stover, resided in Carter County before the war and burned bridges to disrupt Confederate communications. He escaped to Kentucky and began guiding Unionists out of East Tennessee. Ellis later served as captain of Company A, 13th Tennessee Cavalry. After the war, Ellis chronicled his experiences in *The Thrilling Adventures of Captain Dan Ellis, the Great Union Guide of East Tennessee*. This woodcut is from his book.

Life for the Union men left behind Confederate lines could be brutal. This illustration from Ellis's book shows Confederate troops hanging Union men in East Tennessee. Some Unionist troopers took the opportunity to even the score when operating in pro-Confederate areas. (*The Thrilling Adventures of Captain Dan Ellis.*)

This woodcut ("Ellis Piloting a Party Over the Mountains") shows Ellis guiding Union men through the mountains under the cover of darkness. To avoid Confederate home guards, Ellis normally traveled at night along small trails and bridle paths and across physically demanding countryside. More than 4,000 people followed Ellis to Union lines, and over half of them eventually served in the Union army. (*The Thrilling Adventures of Dan Ellis.*)

Scenes such as the one depicted here—"Horrible Scenes from the Rebellion"—were repeated hundreds of times across Tennessee. Tennessee Unionists suffered at the hands of Confederate occupation forces, while Confederated sympathizers suffered retribution from Unionist troops stationed in their midst. As in most wars, the people who suffered the most were the civilians at the mercies of occupying armies. (*The Thrilling Adventures of Dan Ellis.*)

Ellis not only piloted potential soldiers to Union lines, he also carried mail to those already serving in military units from their friends and family who remained in East Tennessee and behind enemy lines. This woodcut ("Ellis Delivering Mail to the Regiment") also shows Union officers studying Confederate fortifications seen by Ellis. (*The Thrilling Adventures of Dan Ellis*.)

This woodcut, entitled "Fight with Vaughn's Rebels," actually portrays the strong division over secession in East Tennessee. The illustration depicts Union men under attack by fellow East Tennessee Confederates commanded by John Crawford Vaughn. Vaughn, a native East Tennessean, commanded Confederate forces stationed in his home region. (*The Thrilling Adventures of Dan Ellis.*)

This stereotypical depiction— "Thomas's Rebel Indians Murdering Union Men"—shows a Union soldier being attacked by William Holland Thomas's Cherokee Legion. Confederate authorities recruited the Legion from among the Eastern Band Cherokees of Tennessee and North Carolina, and they often attacked Unionist civilians and soldiers along the Smoky Mountain chain. Although Thomas's Legion did occasionally don native attire, they hardly looked like the savages depicted at right. (*The Thrilling Adventures of Dan Ellis.*)

THOMAS'S REBEL INDIANS MURDERING UNION MEN.

Daniel Ellis was not the only pilot. Robert Collins guided Union men and operated out of the Cades Cove area of the Smoky Mountains. Confederates killed Collins in 1863. This is his headstone in the Smokies. (GSMNP.)

Cumberland Gap was a natural thoroughfare in the mountain chains located at the junction of Tennessee, Kentucky, and Virginia, and thus had strategic value to both sides. It also served as a gateway for Unionists to escape Confederate Tennessee to safety in Kentucky. Thousands of Tennesseans passed through the gap to join Union regiments forming in Kentucky. (LOC.)

Calvin M. Dyer was a merchant from Granger County before enlisting in Company H, 1st Tennessee, and he rose from private to colonel. When James Brownlow was wounded in 1864, Dyer took over and commanded the regiment during the Tennessee Campaign. He survived the war only to be murdered in 1866 by a black soldier who claimed the colonel insulted him. Dyer's friends captured the soldier, and he was later hanged. (Knox County Two Centuries Photograph Project, McClung Historical Collection.)

Col. Dyer.

yours Respectfuly
W Cook
Lt Col 2nd Ten Cav

William R. Cook served as lieutenant colonel of the 2nd Tennessee Cavalry, and many of his companies formed at Cumberland Gap. The 2nd participated in the Murfreesboro, Tullahoma, and Chickamauga Campaigns. In 1864, the unit took part in the battle of Okolona, Mississippi, and Cook received a sever wound to his neck and was captured. He survived only to be murdered in Kentucky after the war. (TSLA.)

Lt. Col. Robert Galbraith of the 5th Tennessee was a merchant in Shelbyville before the war. He was noted for gallantry in action near his hometown on June 27, 1863. With his unit squabbling over internal leadership issues, Galbraith resigned "to keep harmony" within the unit. The 5th, as Gen. Lovell Rousseau commented, was "neither well drilled, disciplined, or equipped." (John R. Sickles Collection at USAMHI.)

Daniel M. Emerson was 19 years old and of Northern birth when he was appointed major of the 6th Tennessee. Emerson's appointment "against the wishes of the officers and men" made it necessary for him to resign from this West Tennessee Regiment in July 1863. The 6th earned a reputation for violence against Confederate sympathizers. Gen. Nathan Bedford Forrest declared the unit "outlaws and not entitled to be treated as prisoners of war." (John R. Sickles Collection at USAMHI.)

Lt. Col. William H. Ingerton was a veteran of the regular army before being commissioned in the 13th Tennessee Cavalry. During Gillem's campaign in East Tennessee in the summer of 1864, Ingerton received word that Confederate general John Hunt Morgan was sleeping in Greeneville. Ingerton rushed his command into the town and surrounded the Dickson-Williams house. Morgan, one of the most celebrated Confederate cavalry raiders, was shot and killed while trying to escape through the garden. Ingerton later served as a juror on a court martial that found a fellow officer guilty of drunkenness. The guilty officer murdered Ingerton before the war ended. (Roger D. Hunt Collection at USAMHI.)

John H. James served as first lieutenant of Company F, 1st Tennessee, and as regimental quartermaster. In June 1864, he was promoted to captain and assistant quartermaster and acting ordnance officer for all Tennessee troops at the insistence of Governor Johnson. Ultimately, he received a promotion to colonel in the Quartermaster Corps. (Knox County Two Centuries Photograph Project, McClung Historical Collection.)

Joseph Blackburn hailed from DeKalb County and initially commanded a company in the 5th Tennessee Cavalry. In September 1864, Blackburn formed the 4th Tennessee Mounted Infantry with himself as lieutenant colonel. Given the task of wiping out the guerrillas along the Cumberland Plateau, Blackburn waged a heavy-handed campaign against Confederate sympathizers, and his command enticed Champ Ferguson to surrender. After the war, he commanded a company of the State Guard. (Mabry-Charlton Photograph Album, McClung Historical Collection.)

Not all Tennessee Unionists served in regiments from their native state. Col. Frank Wolford commanded the 1st Kentucky Cavalry in battles across the Western Theater. His regiment, as well as many other Kentucky units, included Tennesseans who crossed state lines rather than remain in Confederate territory. (LOC.)

Another Kentuckian with which the Tennessee troopers served was Gen. Richard Johnson. Johnson, an 1849 graduate of the U.S. Military Academy (USMA), served as colonel of the 3rd Kentucky Cavalry before rising to brigade command. Johnson's cavalry brigade included the 3rd Tennessee. As Unionists from slave-holding Southern states, the Kentuckians and Tennesseans had much in common. (LOC.)

The Union cavalry often suffered from poor leadership and mismanagement at the hands of incompetent commanders. There were some notable exceptions. Edward Hatch started the war as a captain in the 2nd Iowa Cavalry but was soon serving as colonel. He participated in a successful raid led by Benjamin Grierson and received promotion to brigadier general. During the Tennessee Campaign of 1864, Hatch ably commanded a division that included the 10th and 12th Tennessee Regiments. He received a brevet for meritorious service during the campaign and a commission as colonel of the 9th U.S. Cavalry at the end of the war. The 9th was one of two cavalry regiments manned by African American enlisted men. (LOC.)

Edward Moody McCook served as colonel of the 2nd Indiana Cavalry. Rising quickly through the ranks, McCook commanded a brigade in the Atlanta Campaign and led a raid south of the city. His command, including the 1st Tennessee, was mauled by the cavalry of Joe Wheeler and William Hicks Jackson as they attempted to return to Union lines. He had 950 men taken prisoner, and he barely escaped capture himself. (LOC.)

Gen. George Stoneman led a raid from the east side of Atlanta that was supposed to rendezvous with McCook and then advance toward Macon and Andersonville to release Union prisoners of war. The disastrous raid resulted in the destruction of his command, and he himself was taken prisoner. Late in the war, he led a raid into East Tennessee, North Carolina, and southwest Virginia that included General Gillem's cavalry brigade. (LOC.)

David Sloane Stanley, an Ohio native and a graduate of the USMA, served as chief of cavalry for the Army of the Cumberland from November 1862 to September 1863. He proved to be a competent commander and instilled confidence in the units under his command. His regiments, including the 5th Tennessee, performed admirably in the Tullahoma Campaign. By 1864, he commanded an infantry corps and was wounded at Franklin. (LOC.)

Gen. William Starke Rosecrans commanded the Army of the Cumberland with great success at Murfreesboro and during the Tullahoma Campaign. Rosecrans wisely placed Gen. David Sloane Stanley in charge of his mounted troops. Rosecrans realized that the occupation and conquest of Tennessee would require vast amounts of mounted troops, and he often complained to the War Department about the quantity and quality of horses supplied to his command. (LOC.)

Samuel Davis Sturgis served in the dragoons and cavalry prior to the Civil War and fought in Missouri, Virginia, and Maryland before arriving in Tennessee. He served as chief of cavalry for the Army of the Ohio and was stationed in Knoxville, where he actively recruited Tennessee regiments. Sent to West Tennessee, Sturgis launched an offensive into Mississippi but was routed by Nathan Bedford Forrest at Brice's Crossroads in June 1864. (LOC.)

Gen. Lovell Harrison Rousseau was a Kentucky native who also lived in Indiana before the war. He first commanded an infantry brigade and later a division in the Army of the Cumberland before commanding the district of Nashville. In the summer of 1864, in support of Sherman's advance on Atlanta, Rousseau led a cavalry raid through Alabama and into Georgia. The 4th Tennessee accompanied Rousseau on this highly successful raid. (LOC.)

Born in Pennsylvania, Joseph Farmer Knipe served in the Mexican War and worked for the Pennsylvania Railroad before the Civil War. He served as colonel of the 46th Pennsylvania Infantry but later commanded an infantry division in the 20th Corps with the rank of brigadier general. Reassigned to the Cavalry Corps, Knipe reported to Memphis to track down and reorganize deserters. He arrived in Nashville in December 1864 and commanded a division of Wilson's cavalry. During the two-day battle of Nashville, his division, which included the 2nd and 4th Tennessee, captured 6,000 men and eight Confederate flags. (LOC.)

James Harrison Wilson graduated from the USMA in 1860. Wilson served as an engineer early in the war and ended up as a staff officer for Gen. U. S. Grant. In February 1864, Wilson took over command of the Cavalry Bureau in Washington and demonstrated his excellent skills as an administrator and organizer. He served briefly under Phil Sheridan in Virginia and was then named Chief of Cavalry of the Military Division of the Mississippi. This placed Wilson in charge of all of the cavalry in the Western theater. Wilson reorganized and reequipped the cavalry and personally led a large portion of his command in the Battle of Nashville. The following spring, Wilson led the largest cavalry force of the Civil War on a raid into Alabama and Georgia. (LOC.)

Gen. Ambrose Burnside was a graduate of the USMA and rose to command the Army of the Potomac, serving in Virginia and Maryland. Reassigned after his disastrous loss at Fredericksburg, Burnside commanded the Department of the Ohio. In September 1863, he successfully marched an army into East Tennessee and occupied Knoxville. The arrival of an army in Knoxville provided an opportunity to recruit more Tennesseans to the Union cause. (LOC.)

Gen. Jacob G. Foster, a USMA graduate and Mexican War veteran, took over the Department of the Ohio from Burnside. Like his predecessor, Foster struggled to maintain order in the highly volatile region of East Tennessee. By the end of 1863, the Union army controlled most of the cities of East Tennessee, yet Confederate commands continued to operate in the countryside, requiring increasing amounts of cavalry to patrol the region. (LOC.)

With guerrilla warfare rampant, Union authorities sent patrols out to curtail outrages against loyal Tennesseans. This photograph shows members of the 3rd Indiana Cavalry who attacked Confederate guerrillas in the Smoky Mountains in 1864. For many years, this photograph was misidentified as scouts of the Army of the Potomac. (LOC.)

HEAD-QUARTERS 9TH ARMY CORPS,

CAMP NEAR KNOXVILLE, TENN., OCT. 19, 1863.

RECRUITS WANTED.

The men of East Tennessee and North Carolina are invited to enlist in the Regiments and Batteries of the 9th Army Corps—General Burnside's old Command.

This celebrated Corps, composed of men from every loyal portion of the Union!—Having served in Virginia, in Maryland, in North and South Carolina, in Mississippi and Kentucky!—Having covered its banners with the mottoes of Victory! —Has now brought its arms to the

DEFENSE OF TENNESSEE.

By enlisting in old Regiments, recruits at once gain all the comforts and convenience possible to a soldier, and are saved from the discomforts, delays, sickness and dangers, arising from ignorance and inexperience, to which all new organizations are subject.

Men enlisting in these Regiments and Batteries, receive the same pay and Bounty as all other recruits; are *at once* clothed, armed, accoutered, comfortably quartered and fed, and placed on the same footing with the old soldiers, and are sure, when it is merited, to win honorable distinction.

They become, almost at once, useful and accomplished soldiers, and save all the inconveniences and loss of time incurred by waiting for the organization of new Regiments, and are sure that their officers are brave, skillful and deserving.

Recruiting parties are established at Knoxville, Morristown, Greeneville and various other points, and *all persons* desiring to join the army, are requested to enlist at once.

By Command of.

BRIG. GEN. ROBT. B. POTTER.

NICOLAS BOWEN,

Asst. Adjt. Gen.

H. BARRY, PRINTER—KNOXVILLE, TENN.

The arrival of a permanent Union force in Knoxville presented the army with its best opportunity to recruit loyal Tennesseans. Gen. Ambrose Burnside's 9th Army Corps generated and distributed this broadside throughout the region and encouraged enlistment in preexisting units. It is believed this surviving example was used in Greeneville. (TSM.)

This photograph, taken during the war, shows Union army tents in the foreground, while across the river, one can see the outskirts of Knoxville and East Tennessee College. The Union army's occupation of Knoxville provided loyal East Tennesseans with a degree of security. However, Confederate cavalry and guerrillas still remained a threat until the end of the war. (LOC.)

Gen. John McAllister Schofield became the final commander of the Department of the Ohio, with his initial headquarters in Knoxville. Schofield, like his predecessors Burnside and Foster, encouraged the Unionists of East Tennessee to join the army and likewise dealt with the guerrillas in the area. Schofield served in the Atlanta Campaign, commanded the Union forces at Franklin, and commanded his 23rd Corps in the Battle of Nashville. (LOC.)

Three

THE TROOPERS
A GALLERY OF ENLISTED MEN

Regiments were only as good as the junior officers, noncommissioned officers, and enlisted men in the ranks. Some Tennessee cavalry regiments were well led, properly equipped, and counted in their ranks devoted and motivated enlisted men. The 1st Tennessee Cavalry, for example, was among the best units the state of Tennessee produced on the Union side. Other units were little more than bushwhackers or guerrillas who received official recognition, weapons, and equipment from the federal government, thus giving some legitimacy to the violent actions aimed at their pro-Confederate neighbors. Nearly all of the Tennessee cavalry regiments spent at least some of their service on anti-guerrilla activity in their home state, which presented ample opportunities for the Union men to exact revenge on their pro-Confederate fellow statesman.

The East Tennessee cavalry regiments, especially those formed prior to 1863, were undoubtedly devoted to the Union cause. With their homes well behind Confederate lines, these men risked their lives, their homes, and their families to make their way along dangerous mountain trails pursued by enemy troops to reach the safety of Union lines simply to enlist. Enlisting was therefore a test of resolve and devotion to the Union cause. Whether these units made good soldiers was debatable, but one could not argue with their dedication. Units from Middle and West Tennessee had an easier physical journey to enlist after the spring of 1862, but they risked ostracism and retribution from the greater number of Confederate sympathizers in their respective areas of the state.

Regardless of whether the units hailed from East, Middle, or West Tennessee, the typical enlisted soldier faced death on a daily basis from guerrillas, normal combat experience, accidents, and disease. The life these men led was extremely difficult. Even in the best of circumstances, the common cavalry soldier spent hours in the saddle on fatigue or guard duty while living on small amounts of poor food and bad water, and all the while living in every type of weather. In general terms, the junior officers, noncommissioned officers, and enlisted men were, depending on the conditions, cold, wet, hot, hungry, homesick, and exhausted.

The images that follow are arranged in regimental order, beginning with the 1st Tennessee Cavalry. Unless otherwise noted, the regiment is referred to by either the number it most commonly used or the number by which it was known late in the war.

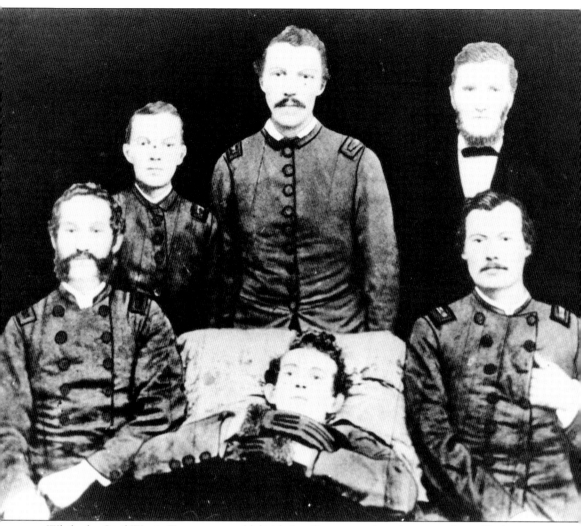

While the Civil War in Tennessee could divide families, more often than not, they rallied to one side or the other. This photograph shows the Kirk family of Greene County. All of the Kirks in the photograph, with the exception of their father, Alexander (wearing the civilian coat at far right), served in the Union army. George (seated at right) served in the 1st Tennessee but returned home to raise his own guerrilla band. Gen. John Schofield authorized Kirk to recruit men for the Union army in 1863, and he raised the 2nd and 3rd North Carolina Mounted Infantry Regiments. James Kirk (standing at center) and John Kirk (seated at left) both served in the 8th Tennessee Cavalry, while William (in the bed) and Francis (standing at left) served in the 3rd and 2nd North Carolina Mounted Infantry Regiments, respectively. Although they had the blessing of the federal government, Kirk's units were little better than guerrillas, and they contributed to the chaos and violence that gripped East Tennessee. (Leon S. Kirk Collection at USAMHI.)

Another Kirk who served the Union cause was Ephriam L. Kirk, who served in Companies C and D, 1st Tennessee. Kirk was a 17-year-old Knox County native and farmer when he enlisted. He spent much of his service as an orderly or escort at division headquarters. (Knox County Two Centuries Photograph Project, McClung Historical Collection.)

Andrew J. Gahagan (or Gohagan) enlisted in Company D, 1st Tennessee at Greeneville and rose from private to first lieutenant. When Capt. George W. Cox was killed at Mossy Creek, Tennessee, in December 1863, Gahagan took over as company commander for the rest of the war. He lived in Chattanooga after the war. (Knox County Two Centuries Photograph Project, McClung Historical Collection.)

55

Capt: J. Lonas.

Jacob K. Lones (or Lonas) served as a private, sergeant, and lieutenant in Company C, 1st Tennessee. When his captain, Elbert Cannon, was killed at Mossy Creek, Lones took command of the company and received a promotion to captain. In March 1864, Lones applied for leave so he could visit his 11-year-old sister in Knoxville, who was suffering from a gunshot wound. His application did not explain how she was wounded. (Knox County Two Centuries Photograph Project, McClung Historical Collection.)

James H. Smith initially served as the orderly sergeant of Company C, 1st Tennessee, but he received a promotion to second lieutenant from Andrew Johnson in July 1864. Smith was wounded during the Battle of Nashville, and one of his comrades, Harrison Collins, received the Medal of Honor for capturing a Confederate flag during the battle. (Knox County Two Centuries Photograph Project, McClung Historical Collection.)

George T. Harris was a house carpenter from Virginia who joined Company I, 1st Tennessee, but later transferred to Company M and served as second lieutenant. Companies L and M were added to the 1st Tennessee after the regiment transferred to cavalry service. The 1st drew horses and received cavalry training at Camp Dennison and Camp Moore, Ohio, in 1862. (Knox County Two Centuries Photograph Project, McClung Historical Collection.)

John Roberts served as a first sergeant in Company C, 1st Tennessee, before receiving a promotion to lieutenant. During McCook's disastrous raid south of Atlanta in July 1864, the 1st Tennessee engaged the cavalry of Joe Wheeler in several fights in an attempt to escape to Union lines. Lieutenant Roberts was killed at Lovejoy Station on July 29, 1864. (Knox County Two Centuries Photograph Project, McClung Historical Collection.)

Martin L. Peters served as first sergeant of Company C, 1st Tennessee Cavalry. Peters survived the war but died after the unit mustered out in 1865. (Knox County Two Centuries Photograph Project, McClung Historical Collection.)

Henry Clay Parham was an 18-year-old farmer from Knox County who served as a corporal in Company C, 1st Tennessee. Parham survived the war and returned to Knoxville. (Knox County Two Centuries Photograph Project, McClung Historical Collection.)

Rufus E. Carson initially served as a private in Company C but mustered out of the regiment in December 1862. He rejoined the regiment at Cumberland Gap in October 1863 and spent most of his service on detached duty as a blacksmith to the ammunition and ambulance trains or at brigade and division headquarters. He lived at Mount Horeb, Tennessee, after the war. (Knox County Two Centuries Photograph Project, McClung Historical Collection.)

Billie Campbell   Ed Mitchell

William "Billie" Campbell and Edward Mitchell both served in Company C, 1st Tennessee. The 1st began the war as the 4th Tennessee Infantry. These men posed wearing untrimmed short jackets and civilian hats. Campbell lived in Lea Park, Tennessee, after the war while Mitchell lived in Elm Park, Oklahoma. (Knox County Two Centuries Photograph Project, McClung Historical Collection.)

James Byron Clapp served as a sergeant in Company C, 1st Tennessee. While pursuing Gen. Joe Wheeler's Confederates in 1864, the 1st Tennessee was heavily engaged near Franklin, Tennessee. Clapp, a Knox County farmer, was carrying the regimental flag when his horse was killed and his leg pinned beneath the animal. He managed to extricate himself with the loss of his boot, but he saved the flag. (Knox County Two Centuries Photograph Project, McClung Historical Collection.)

Byron Clapp.

Brothers Robert A. Adair (left) and John P. Adair both served in Company C, 1st Tennessee. Robert was wounded five times during the war. In November 1864, the 1st fought a delaying action at Sugar Creek, Tennessee. During the fight, Robert received his last wound. With bullets flying about their heads, Sgt. James Byron Clapp and William R. Carter dismounted, recovered the severely wounded soldier, and tossed him across the back of his brother's horse. John received a wound on December 19 during the pursuit of Gen. John B. Hood's retreating army. All four men survived the war. (Knox County Two Centuries Photograph Project, McClung Historical Collection.)

Lindsey & Hodges, KNOXVILLE.

William R. Carter served in Company C, 1st Tennessee. In this carte de visite, Carter appears in the trappings of an infantryman of the 4th Tennessee. After his unit transferred to cavalry service, they received "New suits of blue uniforms, trimmed in yellow, hats ornamented with feathers, and a brass bugle or cross-sabers." After the war, Carter chronicled the regiment's exploits in *History of the First Regiment of Tennessee Volunteer Cavalry*, and he operated a business in Knoxville. (East Tennessee Historical Society.)

This postwar image is reportedly Pvt. Isom (or Isham) Edens, Company G, 1st Tennessee Cavalry. Edens was a farmer from Hancock County. The 1st Tennessee was arguably the best Union cavalry regiment the state produced. The 1st distinguished itself on many battlefields of the Western Theater. (Larry D. Spears Collection at USAMHI.)

James S. McCaluly (or McCaulley) most likely served as private in Company H, 2nd Tennessee Cavalry. A resident of Cades Cove, McCaluly appears in a typical four-button sack coat, wears a regulation saber belt with a revolver tucked into it, and holds another revolver and a cavalry saber. (GSMNP.)

William Goddard was a 21-year-old Blount County farmer when he enlisted in Company H, 2nd Tennessee Cavalry. When attacked by Confederate cavalry near Murfreesboro on December 31, 1862, the 2nd "broke and fled like sheep," according to Col. Lewis Zahm of the 3rd Ohio, but the company redeemed its reputation a month later when it captured three Confederate officers and 41 enlisted men in Middleton, Tennessee. Goddard appears with his wife. (Bobby G. Young Collection at USAMHI.)

This carte de visite is labeled "Major R. H. Dunn" and is most likely Radamanthus H. Dunn of the 2nd Tennessee Infantry Regiment. Many infantry regiments received horses and served, at least temporarily, as mounted infantry. The 2nd Infantry received horses in March 1862 and served mounted until being captured at Rogersville, Tennessee, in November 1863. There is no surviving record of Dunn having served as a major. (TSM.)

This unidentified soldier is believed to be a member of the 2nd Tennessee Mounted Infantry Regiment from Perry County. The corporal posed in a typical infantry frock coat with accoutrements but with mounted service trousers with a reinforced seat. (Scott W. Gilmer.)

Sgt. David H. Walker served in Company D, 2nd Tennessee Infantry, and his regiment received horses in June 1862. While some mounted infantry units served in their infantry clothing and equipment, Walker appears in a cavalry jacket with a Colt revolver and a saber. The 2nd Tennessee Mounted Infantry was composed of men from Middle and West Tennessee and spent much of the war on garrison duty at Clifton, Tennessee. (Wendell G. Walker Collection at USAMHI.)

Riley Graves served in Company B, 3rd Tennessee, at various times as a wagoner and cook. The 3rd Tennessee served in southern Middle Tennessee and north Alabama for much of the war. Nathan Bedford Forrest captured Graves and most of his regiment near Athens, Alabama, in two engagements in 1864. Graves was reported as dead after the *Sultana* explosion, but he mustered out at Camp Chase, Ohio, in May 1865. (Bobbie G. Young Collection at USAMHI.)

William A. McTeer served as lieutenant and adjutant of the 3rd Tennessee Cavalry before serving as acting assistant adjutant general for the 1st Brigade, 4th Cavalry Division, commanded by Col. Jacob Montgomery Thornburgh. While on patrol near Pulaski in September 1864, McTeer suffered from a serious illness and refused to go to the hospital. McTeer wrote of his illness, "Colonel Thornburgh humored my whim, sending an orderly to take care of me until an ambulance came up, then, putting me in it, hauled me along with them. This act of kindness has never been forgotten and never will." McTeer wrote about his experiences, entitled *Among Loyal Mountaineers: The Reminiscences of a Blount County Unionist*, which appeared in the *Knoxville Daily Chronicle*, from February 16, 1879, to April 30, 1880. (TSM.)

Milton Chilcutt served as private, corporal, and sergeant before becoming a lieutenant in Company I, 4th Tennessee Cavalry. Chilcutt was a 40-year-old farmer from Bradley County. During the Battle of Okolona, the brigade commander commented, "The 4th Tennessee acted the whole day with coolness and courage, and never left any position ordered into by the commanding general or myself until outflanked or ordered back." (Thomas G. Clark Collection at USAMHI.)

John R. McCary served in Company B, 4th Tennessee Cavalry. A native of Virginia, McCary joined the regiment in Sullivan County and served with the 4th at Okolona and in McCook's raid south of Atlanta, but he died in a Nashville hospital just before the Battle of Nashville in December 1864. McCary posed with the tools of this trade: a Starr revolver, cavalry saber, and carbine. (Mrs. Ralph Bogart Collection at USAMHI.)

Capt. Hartwell N. T. Shipp commanded Company C, 5th Tennessee Cavalry, and actively participated in the Battle of Murfreesboro and on antiguerrilla operations along the Cumberland Plateau. After the war, Shipp married and lived in Lincoln County. (TSLA.)

In this damaged image, Pvt. John S. Coley, Company K, 5th Tennessee, appears in a regulation cavalry jacket. This 18-year-old native of Cherokee County, Georgia, enlisted in the 5th at Stevenson, Alabama, in late October 1863. Many Unionists joined the first regiments to reach traveling distance regardless of state affiliations. (Mrs. Don C. King Collection at USAMHI.)

The young solider (right) is possibly Jonathan or Isaac Griffith of the 5th Tennessee. Both were cousins of James Griffith (below). The 5th consisted of men from across Middle Tennessee, and they often clashed with Confederate cavalry and guerrillas in the region. James Griffith, like his regimental commander, William B. Stokes, hailed from DeKalb County. Griffith enlisted in Company I, 5th Tennessee, at Murfreesboro and posed wearing his mounted service jacket, saber belt, saber, and Remington "New Model Army" revolver. A superior officer complained that the 5th "is giving me excessive trouble and worrying and plundering through the country whenever they go out. They are under no control or discipline, as far as I can learn. Several instances have come to my hearing of their insulting unprotected females. I could not learn the names of the guilty parties." (Both, TSM.)

ROBERT. H LOCK.
JULIA. A LOCK.

The Union army raised the 6th Tennessee Cavalry from among loyal men in West Tennessee with Fielding Hurst as colonel; they operated in that section of the state for most of the war. The unit earned a reputation for abusing pro-Confederates. Cpl. Robert H. Lock, a farmer in McNairy County, appears with his wife, Julia. Lock enlisted in September 1863 and served until discharged at Pulaski in 1865. (Courtesy of Dr. Doug Locke.)

Walter Gregory hailed from Cades Cove and enlisted in the 6th Tennessee Infantry. Although not in a cavalry regiment, Gregory's story demonstrates the experience of many loyalists. While away serving with his regiment, Gregory's father was murdered by Confederate guerrillas on the home front. Walter died while in service. (GSMNP.)

The 7th Tennessee was composed of West Tennessee Unionists and surrendered to Nathan Bedford Forrest on two different occasions. Pvt. Joseph Riley Ward was captured at Trenton in 1862 and paroled, only to be captured again at Union City in March 1864. He spent most of the next year at the prison camp at Andersonville, Georgia, where he contracted scurvy. He survived the war and returned to Carroll County. (Carl M. Ward Collection at USAMHI.)

Pvt. Stephen N. Clement (or Clemons) joined Company D, 7th Tennessee, in January 1864 at Paris, Tennessee. Clement was with the regiment for only a few months when the regiment surrendered at Union City. Sent to Andersonville, Clement survived but suffered from poor health for the rest of his life because of the horrid conditions of the overcrowded prison camp. (Mrs. Anita C. Collins Collection at USAMHI.)

Some Union men initially served in the Confederate army because of state allegiance, fear of reprisals, or forced conscription. The Bible family provided nine soldiers to the 61st Tennessee Infantry (Confederate). By August 1863, all of them had died, deserted, or joined Union regiments. John C. Bible was captured in Mississippi and decided that Union service was preferable to prison. He joined Company A, 8th Tennessee Cavalry (Union) and ultimately commanded Company G in Tennessee, Virginia, and North Carolina. (R. Donahue Bible Collection at USAMHI.)

Capt. George Edgar Grisham commanded Company I, 8th Tennessee Cavalry. He kept a photo album that included many images of his regiment that were taken while stationed near Gallatin in the summer of 1864. This ferrotype of Grisham was taken at Camp Nelson, Kentucky, in November 1863. Grisham was a devout Union man and edited a newspaper in Jonesborough before and after the war. (TSM.)

The only photograph of a female in Grisham's album was this tintype of his wife, Maggie. Grisham sent her the photo album and inscribed a poem to her in the front. The poem reads: *"To My Wife,/ Tho far from thy side and by dangers surrounded,/ Tho the battle-cry is not the theme of my life,/ There dwells in my heart a sweet feeling of gladness,/ That God will restore thee to me-loving wife-G.E.G. May 29, 1864."* The Grishams lost two children during the war, and George resigned his commission in October 1864 and returned home. (TSM.)

Grisham's album contained carte de visites of many regimental and company officers. First Lt. Spencer Munson served as the regimental adjutant until he resigned in January 1865. The adjutant kept all of the regiment's written records and assisted the colonel with preparing written orders. (TSM.)

The quartermaster of a cavalry regiment was not only responsible for clothing the troopers in his command, but also had the task of providing feed for the horses. Lt. Henry A. Kelly was the acting assistant quartermaster until May 13, 1864. The following day, Kelly was officially appointed regimental quartermaster. (TSM.)

John Sharp served as the second lieutenant of Company B before taking over command as captain. Sharp appears in a military-style vest with his pocket watch. He resigned his commission in January 1865. (TSM.)

Capt. David Rush's Company B, 8th Tennessee, included men from Hawkins, Greene, and Jefferson Counties. In October 1864, Captains Rush and William J. S. Denton led the 3rd Squadron of the 8th on a scouting mission, which resulted in a skirmish near Greeneville. In this skirmish, Confederate mounted units from East Tennessee led by John Crawford Vaughn captured a flag from the 8th. (TSM.)

The occupation of Knoxville in September 1863 by Burnside's Corps allowed for increased recruiting among the Unionist populace. Company D, 8th Tennessee, organized in November 1863 and consisted of men from Washington, Greene, Hawkins, Hamblen, and Cocke Counties. Josiah Mahoney was appointed second lieutenant on July 1, 1864. (TSM.)

Capt. Lewis Jarvis was 34 years old and commanded Company E, 8th Tennessee. Company E formed in Sneedville in the summer of 1863 and consisted of men from Hancock County. Jarvis resigned his commission on March 16, 1865. (TSM.)

Some of the units that would eventually form the 8th Tennessee did not wait for Union forces to arrive but instead made their way to Kentucky. Company F organized at Camp Nelson, Kentucky, in August 1863 and consisted of men from Greene, Washington, Carter, Hamilton, Union, and Knox Counties. Fielding L. McVay was appointed captain on May 26, 1864, having first served as lieutenant. (TSM.)

Capt. Christopher C. Kenner organized Company G, 8th Tennessee, at Somerset, Kentucky, in July 1863. Kenner received a promotion to major of the regiment in March 1865. Records suggest Kenner may have previously served as a sergeant in Frank Wolford's 1st Kentucky Cavalry. (TSM.)

Daniel D. Markwood joined Company H, 8th Tennessee, as a private but was appointed captain in July 1865. Although the last major Confederate armies surrendered in April and May 1865, the 8th Tennessee did not muster out until September. The regiment spent the intervening months attempting to restore order to war-ravaged East Tennessee. (TSM.)

William J. S. Denton served as lieutenant and captain of Company H, 8th Tennessee, but he was later promoted to major. In October 1864, Captains Denton and David Rush commanded a scouting expedition near Greeneville and lost a unit flag to capture at the hands of the Confederates. A month later, Confederates captured Denton's personal papers during a surprise raid. (TSM.)

Capt. George Grisham's album included this carte de visite of himself. Grisham had several patriotic poems published in East Tennessee papers extolling the beauty of his home state and adherence to the Union. Grisham wrote in the album the following: "I am for putting down this Rebellion, let it cost what it may, in Treasure and in Blood—the utter subjugation, and, if need be, extermination of all Traitors! I am for the Union first—I am for the Union last—I am for the Union in life and in death—In Time and in Eternity—I am for the freedom of all human beings!" Grisham resigned his commission in October 1864 but commanded a company of the State Guard, which struggled to control the chaos and the Ku Klux Klan in Tennessee during Reconstruction. (TSM.)

Lt. James P. Kendrick took over command of Company I, 8th Tennessee, after Captain Grisham's resignation. Kendrick (also Kindrick) received a promotion to captain on March 18, 1865, and commanded the company for the remainder of the war. (TSM.)

This image shows Lt. Enoch Brown (seated) of Company I, 8th Tennessee, and three enlisted men identified as Brown's "Bodyguard." The three enlisted men are (from left to right) John Archer, Sgt. James Matthew Martin, and Cpl. Anthony G. Hamilton. All of the men appear in civilian-style slouch hats and with their sabers and saber belts. Archer and Hamilton wear fatigue sack coats, while Martin wears a standard mounted jacket. (TSM.)

John W. McCoy served as private and later lieutenant in Company L, 8th Tennessee. In March 1865, he was appointed as captain and commanded Company K.

Company M, 8th Tennessee, mustered in Nashville in March 1864 with Nelson McLaughlin as captain. With the war over, many officers resigned their commissions and returned home. McLaughlin resigned in June 1865. In this carte de visite, McLaughlin carries an infantry officer's sword and wears a nonregulation militia-style belt plate. (TSM.)

Captain Grisham labeled this image "Sergeants of Co. 'I' 8th Tenn. Cav. Vols." and identified the soldiers (from left to right) as Orderly Sergeant A. M. Stuart, Commissary Sergeant Theodore Bowman, Quartermaster Sergeant John B. Hartman, and 4th Sgt. Samuel Dykes. Interestingly, none of the sergeants wear chevrons. The company guidon is visible just above Sergeant Hartman. (TSM.)

Most of these sergeants in Company I appear with chevrons. Standing are Nathan Shipley (left) and Mathias K. Hale (right). First Sergeant Shipley went missing in action in November 1864 and was listed as a deserter. In reality, Shipley was a prisoner of war. He escaped and returned to his unit in April 1865. Hale was wounded at Morristown in October 1864 and spent the rest of the war in the hospital. Seated are John C. Britt, with his saber, and Nathan Simpson, with his Colt "Army" revolver. (TSM.)

Elihu R. Owings originally served as the orderly sergeant for Company I, 8th Tennessee, but he requested to be reduced to private. He later served as a clerk to Tennessee adjutant general Alvan Gillem. In November 1864, Owings received a promotion to lieutenant and regimental quartermaster of the 4th Tennessee Mounted Infantry Regiment. (TSM.)

James Henry Miller (seated) served as a lieutenant in Company A, 8th Tennessee. He appears in this photograph with J. A. R. Nelson, presumably also of the 8th Tennessee. (TSM.)

Both James S. Hale (standing) and
Landon C. Chase were members of Company I,
8th Tennessee. Hale, according to comments in
Grisham's album, served as the colonel's orderly.
Hale was an 18-year-old farmer and was listed
as 5 feet, 4½ inches tall. He later served as a
sergeant. Landon Chase was a 24-year-old farmer
from Washington County who spent part of his
service attached to the brigade hospital. (TSM.)

Elijah Carey served as a sergeant in
Company I, 8th Tennessee. Carey
wears a privately purchased sack coat
and proudly displays his sergeant
chevrons. Some Union soldiers
purchased coats that mimicked
the issue sack coat but had custom
features such as exterior pockets and
additional buttons. (TSM.)

Pictured here are some of the corporals of Company I, 8th Tennessee. Seated are James Ratliff (left) and John W. Leab. Ratliff later became a lieutenant in Company D. Leab is holding his Colt "Army" revolver. Standing behind Ratliff is James Hix, who is sporting a light-colored civilian hat and showing his Remington revolver. Standing next to Hix is David G. W. Barnes Jr. Barnes's father was also in Company I. (TSM.)

David G. W. Barnes Sr. was a 44-year-old tailor when he enlisted in 1863. According to George Grisham, Barnes was known in the regiment as "Tar Water." Barnes deserted the regiment in July 1864 and returned to his company only to desert again in May 1865. He was restored to duty by order of Gen. Alvan Gillem. (TSM.)

Grisham referred to this man as Dr. Jacob Leab of Company I, 8th Tennessee. This is probably the same Jacob Leab who received an appointment to lieutenant and regimental adjutant in March 1865. (TSM.)

Archibald Vanderenter was a 42-year-old farmer from Sullivan County who served in Company I, 8th Tennessee. Although listed as a private, Vanderenter sports an officer's-style hat cord, and records indicate he provided his own horse and horse equipage rather than using a government-issued horse and saddle. (TSM.)

From left to right, Pvt. Thomas H. McLaine, blacksmith Michael H. Martin, blacksmith E. E. Ferguson, and saddler A. J. Shupe, all of Company I, 8th Tennessee, appear in this rare image. Most cavalry regiments used specialized and skilled laborers such as blacksmiths and saddlers to maintain their horses and equipment. These men posed with the tools of their much-in-demand trades. Blacksmiths spent countless hours doing the backbreaking work of shoeing horse and mules. The saddler is shown with a "Texas" saddle tree, a style atypical of Union forces. (TSM.)

These three men were all members of Captain Grisham's company. Standing is James Smith, while the two men seated are Privates Samuel Bowman (left) and William Clark. Smith and Clark both wear typical mounted service jackets, while Bowman appears in a fatigue sack coat. (TSM.)

These two young men are James Short (left) and Adam Bacon of Company I, 8th Tennessee. There were three Bacon men who served in Company I. (TSM.)

James F. Moore, of Company I, 8th Tennessee, wears a regulation cavalry mounted services jacket along with his saber, carbine, and two Colt Army revolvers thrust into his saber belt. Captured near Marion, Virginia, in November 1864, Moore escaped from his captors and returned to his unit in May 1865. He was known in his company as "General Moore." (TSM.)

These four members represent the hard-riding volunteers of the 8th Tennessee who would take the war to the Confederates in 1864 and 1865 in East Tennessee, southwest Virginia, and western North Carolina. Seated are Joseph Mitchell (left) and William B. Ball. Standing behind them are brothers William K. Jones (left) and Samuel Jones. Samuel Jones sports a large neckerchief. (TSM.)

This image shows Andrew Shupe (left) and William Case. Shupe was the saddler of Company I, 8th Tennessee, and he also appears in the photograph of the artificers of the company on page 92. Case served as a private. (TSM.)

These two young men were also members of the 8th Tennessee. The standing soldier is William R. Phillips, and the seated one is John M. Bails; both wear issue fatigue sack coats and civilian slouch hats. Phillips has his company letter, "I," on his hat. (TSM.)

Cavalry units operated, maneuvered, and fought by the sound of the bugle. Samuel B. Rushbrooks served as a bugler in the 8th Tennessee. Beneath his photograph, Captain Grisham wrote, "Bugler of our Company and Son of Wm. Rushbrook Drygood Merchant, No. 94, Main Street, Richmond, Virginia. Known in the Regt. As "Beauregard." Rushbrook wears a fatigue cap, collarless shirt, an untrimmed shell jacket, and a civilian checked vest. (TSM.)

Standing are privates Andrew Sherfey (left) and Murry B. Lain. Both men wore black or dark-colored civilian slouch hats and their saber belts without the shoulder strap. Sherfey wears a sack coat. The seated soldiers are Jesse Hunt (left) and George W. Brooks, who wear light-colored civilian slouch hats, army-issued mounted service jackets, and saber belts. (TSM.)

Privates Robert Greggs (left) and John P. Taylor of Company I, 8th Tennessee, appear in this photograph. The young Greggs altered his issue mounted service jacket by adding an exterior pocket. Also visible is a ring on his pinky finger. (TSM.)

Little information remains concerning the service of Easton M. Woods of Company I, 8th Tennessee. Grisham wrote beneath Woods's photograph, "Known in the Co. as "Gen. Woods." Before the arrival of Union troops, Confederate authorities conscripted many loyal Tennesseans into their armies. The Easton Woods seen here may have initially served in Company D, 63rd Tennessee Infantry (Confederate). (TSM.)

These dashing members of the 8th Tennessee are, from left to right, Calvin Hix, Henry M. Walker, and William Cox. All three men wear civilian slouch hats and mounted service jackets. (TSM.)

Lilburn W. DePugh (left), David Hays (standing), and Andrew J. Campbell (right) also served in Company I, 8th Tennessee. DePugh wears a light-colored civilian slouch hat and proudly displays his .50-caliber Smith breech-loading carbine, the fourth most commonly issued cavalry long-arm. Campbell modified his issue jacket by adding an exterior breast pocket, while Hays appears in the typical fatigue sack coat. (TSM.)

These three members of the 8th Tennessee are James Ford (left), James Calvin Epperson (center), and John A. Ford (right). James Ford wears an issue sack coat that appears to be a little small for his large frame. He also wears an issue "Hardee" hat with brass cavalry insignia affixed. John Ford also wears a "Hardee" hat, while Epperson has a civilian slouch hat. (TSM.)

Proudly displaying their sabers are privates Albert M. Owings (standing, left), James C. Cheatham (standing, right), Andrew J. Potter (seated, left), and Samuel Mullins (seated, right). Potter has turned down the lapels of his mounted service jacket to display a checked civilian shirt and a neckerchief. (TSM.)

Pvt. William R. Settle, Company I, 8th Tennessee Cavalry, proudly displays his .44-caliber Colt "Army" revolver while wearing the typical Union fatigue coat, forage cap, and knee-high nonregulation riding boots. A saddler before the war, Settle was detached to the brigade ambulance corps in the summer of 1864. (TSM.)

Company I, 8th Tennessee Cavalry, posed for this photograph near Gallatin, Tennessee, on June 29, 1864. Captain Grisham stands in the middle of the photograph with the company guidon just behind him. The men appear in a mixture of sack coats and mounted service jackets, slouch hats and forage caps, with saber belts and Smith carbines. (TSM.)

Photographs of men on horseback were especially rare because the long exposure time required a horse to stand still for at least 30 seconds. Captain Grisham, pointing his sword, described the image: "Capt. Geo. Edgar Grisham, Co. 'I,' 8th Tenn. Cav. Vols. As Field Officers of the Day, 3rd Brig., 4th Divis. Cav. Corps./ Camp near Gallatin, Tenn./ June 27th, 1864/ Instructing to the Officer of the Guard/ Lieut. Henry Jackson, Co. 'E,' 9th Tenn. Cav. Vols. Officer of the Guard." (TSM.)

Twenty-five-year-old David M. Caldwell received his appointment as captain of Company B, 9th Tennessee, on December 20, 1863. Company B consisted of men from Claiborne, Union, Knox, Jefferson, and Rhea Counties. The 9th served predominately in Gen. Alvan Gillem's "Governor's Guard" in East and Middle Tennessee and participated in the attack on Greeneville in 1864, which resulted in the death of John Hunt Morgan. (TSM.)

Jacob Fritts served as lieutenant in Company B, 11th Tennessee Cavalry. After the consolidation of the 9th and the 11th regiments, Fritts served as captain of Company H, 9th Tennessee Cavalry Regiment. (TSM.)

The War Department consolidated the 9th and 11th Tennessee Regiments in March 1865, and many officers are thus listed as having served in both regiments. For example, William B. Robbins of Sullivan County is listed as both the first lieutenant of Company I of the 9th and Company C of the 11th. In 1863, the 11th served predominately near Cumberland Gap. Gen. Kenner Garrard complained of the 11th that "the 11th Tennessee Cavalry [have] 252 men for duty, no horses, are without discipline, and with their present organization [are] of but little value." (TSM.)

William A. Crouch joined Company C, 9th Tennessee, in August 1863 and served with the regiment in operations in East and Middle Tennessee until hospitalized with measles in 1864. Upon recovery, he received a promotion to corporal and fought with his regiment against the Confederate cavalry under John Hunt Morgan, Basil Duke, and John Crawford Vaughn. Crouch shows off his Remington "Army" revolver in this photograph. (Dorothy May Hugh Collection at USAMHI.)

John C. Wright was from Fentress County and joined Company D, 11th Tennessee, in August 1863 at Camp Nelson, Kentucky. He served as the provost marshal at Cumberland Gap in late 1864. After the consolidation of the two regiments, Wright served briefly as captain of Company G, 9th Tennessee, before receiving a promotion to major near the war's end. (TSM.)

This postwar photograph shows Jesse V. Lutrell from Greene County, who served originally as private in Company L, 11th Tennessee. With the consolidation of the regiments, Luttrell received a promotion to corporal in Company M, 9th Tennessee. (Francis H. Luttrell Collection at USAMHI.)

Charles C. Hoefling served in the 4th U.S. Cavalry before joining the 12th Tennessee in January 1864 and rose to lieutenant colonel. The 12th guarded rail lines around Nashville until they ran into Gen. Nathan B. Forrest's cavalry near Spring Hill in October 1864. Hoefling delayed the advancing Confederates but was wounded in the process and resigned in January 1865. During the Battle of Nashville, the 12th captured Gen. Edmund Rucker and the wagon train of Gen. James Chalmers. (John R. Sickles Collection at USAMHI.)

The 12th Tennessee served for several months after most hostilities ceased. The unit operated predominately in Tennessee, Alabama, and Mississippi before spending the last months of enlistment in Kansas and Missouri. This postwar image shows Jesse C. Ellis of Company C, 12th Tennessee. Ellis deserted from a Nashville hospital in March 1864 but returned to the unit to be mustered out at Fort Leavenworth, Kansas, in September 1865. (Mrs. J. R. Cornelius Sr. Collection at USAMHI.)

Company I, 12th Tennessee, consisted mostly of men from states other than Tennessee. Pvt. Henry B. Couch enrolled in the regiment on March 5, 1864, at Pikeville, Tennessee, but listed his home as Canton, Georgia. Couch served as a bugler and deserted the regiment near St. George, Kansas, on June 23, 1865. (M. Beverly Erickson Collection at USAMHI.)

Jacob P. Crooker was 22 years old when he enlisted as lieutenant of Company I, 12th Tennessee, in Nashville. Promoted to captain, Crooker served as the provost marshal of the 5th Division of the Cavalry Corps. Crooker probably had firsthand knowledge of the provost marshal's job, as his records indicate he was drunk for two or three days in June 1864 while in Nashville. (John R. Sickles Collection at USAMHI.)

Lt. Alfred C. Williams was a native of Stoney Creek, Tennessee, and served in Company F, 13th Tennessee Cavalry. The 13th served in East Tennessee and participated in the attack on Greeneville, which resulted in the death of John Hunt Morgan. Williams missed this fight because he resigned his commission on August 27, 1864. He died in Carter County in 1900. (TSLA.)

Cpl. William H. Albritton joined Bradford's 13th West Tennessee (also known as the 14th Tennessee) in 1863. The unit received orders "to impress horses from both the loyal and the disloyal." When Gen. Nathan B. Forrest threatened Fort Pillow, the 268 men of the 14th assisted the 6th U.S. Colored Artillery in the defense. Two-thirds of the garrison were either killed or captured when Forrest attacked. William Albritton escaped with a wound to the arm that resulted in its amputation. (Shirley Wagner Collection at USAMHI.)

Some Unionists served in units that were not officially part of the army. The two men pictured here are Jonathan D. Hale (left) and "Tinker Dave" Beaty, both of Fentress County. Hale, a native of New Hampshire, served as the postmaster in Fentress County but fled to Kentucky upon Tennessee's secession. He raised a small unit of scouts and served as the chief of scouts for the Army of the Cumberland. During Reconstruction, he served as a physician in the State Guard. Beaty similarly raised an independent scout unit and waged a brutal brand of guerrilla warfare against Confederate irregulars under Champ Ferguson. Beaty received at least three wounds during the war, and his men received no pay. He later became a prominent Republican in Fentress County. (MOLLUS Collection at USAMHI.)

Many Tennessee cavalry regiments spent months patrolling hundreds of miles of vulnerable rail lines that ran through Tennessee, Alabama, Mississippi, and Georgia. This photograph was taken along the Nashville and Chattanooga Railroad. Visible just beyond the railroad cars are several unidentified Union cavalrymen. (LOC.)

To protect the vulnerable railroads from guerrillas and Confederate cavalry, the Union army built blockhouses along the lines. These blockhouses were garrisoned by small detachments, which often included cavalry or mounted infantry units. Significant portions of the 3rd Tennessee Cavalry found themselves surrounded and forced to surrender while defending a stretch of the Nashville and Decatur Railroad in north Alabama in 1864. The blockhouse in this photograph was located along the Nashville and Chattanooga Railroad. (LOC.)

Undoubtedly the most horrific of the Confederate prison camps was Andersonville in south Georgia. Nearly every Tennessee cavalry regiment had at least one trooper imprisoned at Andersonville, and more than 1,500 Tennessee soldiers were confined in the prison during the war. This image shows the crude shelters erected by the prisoners for protection from the elements. (LOC.)

The prison camp at Cahaba, Alabama, was located in an abandoned cotton warehouse and was prone to flooding and extreme overcrowding. However, prisoners at Cahaba fared better than those at other camps. Members of the 3rd Tennessee captured at Athens and Sulphur Branch Trestle, Alabama, spent much of their captivity at Cahaba. (LOC.)

Four

THE POSTWAR YEARS AND THE LEGACY

By 1864, some Americans doubted that the Union could win the war. The presidential election of 1864 saw the "Peace Democrat" George B. McClellan receive his party's nomination. McClellan's platform called for an immediate cessation of hostilities and recognition of Southern independence. Not all Democrats supported the peace candidate, and the leading opponent was Andrew Johnson. Abraham Lincoln, a Republican, in an effort to reach across party lines and to ensure the preservation of the Union, chose Johnson as his vice presidential running mate.

The fall of Atlanta to Gen. William T. Sherman's army in September 1864, combined with the mixed-party presidential ticket, won Lincoln a second term, and he lived to see Gen. Robert E. Lee surrender and the beginning of the reunification of the nation. However, Lincoln's assassination propelled Johnson into the White House. Johnson suddenly was president yet did not enjoy the support of either political party: the Republicans, especially the Radicals, refused to support the Democrat, while "Peace Democrats" resented Johnson's tie to the Republicans. Furthermore, Congress was sharply divided over the plans for reconstructing the South at the war's conclusion. Johnson favored a lenient plan of reconstruction to more rapidly reunify the nation. Meanwhile, many of the Radical Republicans sought a vindictive plan to punish the South. Due to his reluctance to go along with the Radicals, Johnson was impeached. He was found innocent by a single vote and finished out the remainder of Lincoln's term. He eventually returned to the Senate, representing Tennessee.

Reconstruction was difficult for all Southerners, including former Union soldiers. Many returned home to find their farms destroyed, their livestock stolen, and their families missing. Some feared retribution from pro-Confederate neighbors for the rest of their lives. As time passed, some scars of the recent war faded. Unfortunately, so too did the actions and contributions of Tennessee's Unionist cavalrymen. After Reconstruction, many promoted the ideas of the heroic Confederates fighting against all odds to maintain the Old South ways. The "Lost Cause" mentality allowed no room for Southern loyalists in the interpretation of history. This contributed to the erasing from the collective memory the contributions of the Tennessee Union men. Furthermore, the brutality of Gov. William Brownlow during Reconstruction gave reason for many Southerners to resent these loyal cavaliers.

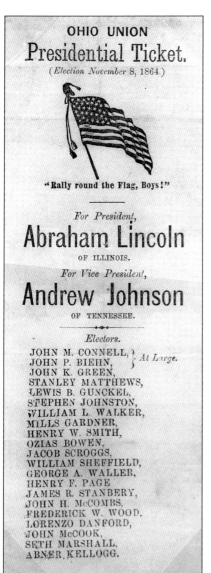

OHIO UNION
Presidential Ticket.
(Election November 8, 1864.)

"Rally round the Flag, Boys!"

For President,
Abraham Lincoln
OF ILLINOIS.

For Vice President,
Andrew Johnson
OF TENNESSEE.

Electors.

JOHN M. CONNELL, ⎱ *At Large.*
JOHN P. BIEHN, ⎰
JOHN K. GREEN,
STANLEY MATTHEWS,
LEWIS B. GUNCKEL,
STEPHEN JOHNSTON,
WILLIAM L. WALKER,
MILLS GARDNER,
HENRY W. SMITH,
OZIAS BOWEN,
JACOB SCROGGS,
WILLIAM SHEFFIELD,
GEORGE A. WALLER,
HENRY F. PAGE
JAMES R. STANBERY,
JOHN H. McCOMBS,
FREDERICK W. WOOD,
LORENZO DANFORD,
JOHN McCOOK,
SETH MARSHALL,
ABNER KELLOGG.

In an effort to win support for continuing the war effort, Lincoln reached across party lines and selected a Southern Democrat as his vice presidential running mate. This is a presidential election ballot from the election of 1864 from the state of Ohio. (TSM.)

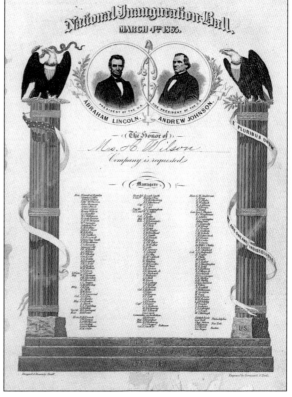

With the fall of Atlanta to Sherman in September 1864, most Americans viewed the war as winnable, and Lincoln won reelection. Pictured at right is an invitation to the inauguration ball for Abraham Lincoln and Andrew Johnson. Just over a month after the inauguration, Lincoln would be assassinated and Johnson would be president. (TSM.)

As the war approached its conclusion, Union prisoners of war began to make their way from the horrors of prison camps toward their homes. This photograph is of the steamboat *Sultana* docked near Helena, Arkansas, on the Mississippi River. The *Sultana*'s decks were overloaded with soldiers who survived Andersonville and Cahaba. Many of the men seen on the decks would die within days of this photograph being taken. (LOC.)

The *Sultana*, loaded well beyond capacity with former prisoners of war, moved up the Mississippi River in April 1865. On April 27, just north of Memphis, one of her boilers exploded. An estimated 1,800 of the 2,400 passengers died in the deadliest maritime disaster in American history. More than 600 Unionist Tennessee soldiers, most of them members of the 3rd Tennessee Cavalry, were killed in the disaster. (Woodcut from *Harper's Weekly*, LOC.)

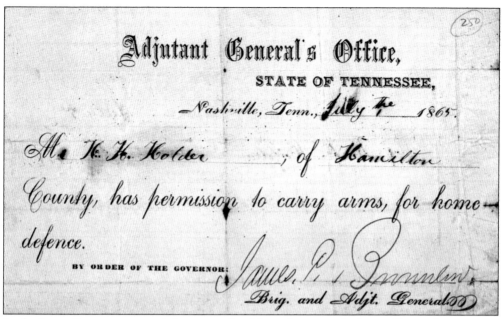

Adjutant General's Office,

STATE OF TENNESSEE,

Nashville, Tenn., July 4th 1865.

Mr. H. H. Holder ; of Hamilton County, has permission to carry arms, for home defence.

BY ORDER OF THE GOVERNOR: James P. Brownlow,

Brig. and Adjt. General.

In the immediate postwar period, as a result of fear of a renewal of guerrilla warfare, citizens needed permission to carry firearms. James P. Brownlow served as adjutant general of Tennessee during Reconstruction. His father, William, was Tennessee's Reconstruction governor and was noted for his harsh treatment of former Confederate supporters. James married the daughter of a former Confederate surgeon from Williamson County. He died of tuberculosis in 1879. (TSM.)

William Brickle Stokes formed the 5th Tennessee Cavalry and waged a brutal campaign against Confederate troops and guerrillas. After the war, he served as a Republican congressman and unsuccessfully ran for governor. This cane was presented to Colonel Stokes after the war and is inscribed, "From the Union Men of Tennessee to Col. WMB. Stokes/ A union man who loves the brethren/ Feby. 22nd/ 1866." (TSM.)

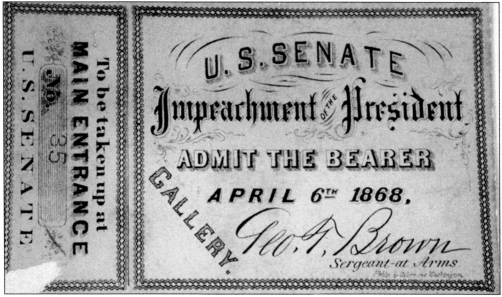

Abraham Lincoln's assassination propelled Andrew Johnson into the presidency. Johnson, a Southern Democrat, spared continuously with Radical Republicans over the plan of Reconstruction and the criteria by which Southern states could be restored to the Union. By 1868, political warfare raged out of control between the president and the Radicals, and the House voted for impeachment. The impeachment hearing in the Senate was the cause célèbre. Tickets, like the one above, were required to witness the hearings. Ultimately, Johnson was acquitted by the Senate by a single vote, and he remained in office, but his political power was greatly diminished. The Democrats did not renominate him, and he returned to Tennessee. (TSM.)

Former Confederates were disenfranchised and harshly treated by Radicals such as Tennessee's Reconstruction governor, William Brownlow. Some former soldiers formed the Ku Klux Klan to deal with the Radicals, to discourage black voters, and to protect the rights of former Confederates. Klansman used violence and fear to control the freed blacks and to intimidate carpetbaggers. (Woodcut from *Harper's Weekly*, LOC.)

To control the Klan and to maintain order during Reconstruction, Governor Brownlow used the Tennessee State Guard. Gen. Joseph A. Cooper, a Tennessee Unionist general, commanded the guard and tried to be even-handed. Former Tennessee cavalrymen commanded nine of the Tennessee State Guard companies. (LOC.)

William Farrand Prosser came to Tennessee as part of the 15th Pennsylvania Cavalry but transferred to the 2nd Tennessee Cavalry and became colonel. He was commended for his actions at the Battle of Decatur by Gen. Gordon Granger. After the war, Prosser served in the House of Representatives and later moved to Washington state, and served as a delegate to the constitutional convention. The town of Prosser, Washington, is named in his honor. (LOC.)

Jacob Montgomery Thornburgh, an attorney in Jefferson County, enlisted in the 4th Tennessee Cavalry as private but rose to the rank of lieutenant colonel. At Okolona, Mississippi, the unit was noted for its coolness under fire. The 4th participated in the Atlanta, Tennessee, and Mobile Campaigns in 1864–1865. After the war, Thornburgh served as the attorney general of the third circuit. He served in the U.S. House of Representatives from 1873 until 1879 and retired from public life in 1880. (LOC.)

James H. Haney enrolled in Company G, 11th Tennessee Cavalry, at Knoxville as soon as Gen. Ambrose Burnside's Army of the Ohio arrived in the city. Haney is pictured here proudly wearing his membership badge of the Grand Army of the Republic. The Grand Army of the Republic, or GAR, was the largest organization of Civil War veterans. At its height in the 1890s, it counted more than 500,000 members with posts across the country. Tennessee's Union cavalry veterans were eligible for membership, and several posts were located in Tennessee. (Howard Haney Collection at USAMHI.)

Noah Abbott served in the 9th Tennessee Cavalry as private and corporal, and survived the war to return to his home in Cades Cove. Abbott appears in this photograph wearing his GAR ribbons and holding his hunting rifle. In the postwar years, many former Tennessee Union soldiers joined the GAR. (GSMNP.)

The GAR became the largest Union Civil War veteran's organization. The GAR supported veterans' reunions but also lobbied for benefits and for the protection of veterans' pensions. With hundreds of thousands of members nationwide, the GAR wielded much political power. This poster illustrates the virtues of the organization: Loyalty to the Union, fraternity among Union veterans, and charity in assisting veterans and the widows and orphans of deceased veterans. (LOC.)

Part of the mission of the GAR was to provide assistance to the widows and children of deceased Union veterans. Ribbons like the one pictured here were often worn to assist in fund-raising efforts for the GAR. The original owner of this ribbon is unknown. (TSM.)

Many Union veterans and their families attended reunions of their units in the decades after the war. This ribbon is from the 1st Tennessee Cavalry Regiment and belonged to a member of the Brownlow family. James Patton Brownlow served as the colonel of the 1st, but he died in 1879. (TSM.)

Samuel Powahatan Carter served on detached duty with the army commanding cavalry for much of the Civil War. After the war, Carter returned to his career in the U.S. Navy and ultimately obtained the rank of admiral. This distinguished Tennessee Unionist is the only man in American history to obtain the rank of army general and navy admiral. In this portrait, Carter appears in his post–Civil War admiral's uniform. (TSM.)

This is a postwar photograph of Sgt. Edmond B. Sampley of Company B, 1st Alabama and Tennessee Vidette Cavalry. Sampley, a resident of McMinn County, joined his unit at Stevenson, Alabama, in September 1863. The 1st Alabama and Tennessee consisted of Union men from Tennessee, Alabama, and Georgia and generally operated as scouts for the Union army. The unit should not be confused with the 1st Tennessee Cavalry. (Mrs. Don C. King Collection at USAMHI.)

David Taylor, Company H, 4th Tennessee, enlisted at the age of 33 in Greeneville and listed his occupation as blacksmith. Taylor was listed as "sick in hospital with jaundice" in November and December 1864. He apparently recovered and accompanied his unit on the Mobile Campaign when, in March 1865, he was again admitted to an army hospital. He survived the war and posed with his wife for this photograph later in life. (J. Howard Morelock Collection at USAMHI.)

James Griffith survived his service with the 5th Tennessee Cavalry and returned to DeKalb County in Middle Tennessee after the war. Griffith, like most Union veterans in Tennessee, tried to resume his life and obtain some degree of normalcy. This is the remembrance card from Griffith's funeral in 1924. (TSM.)

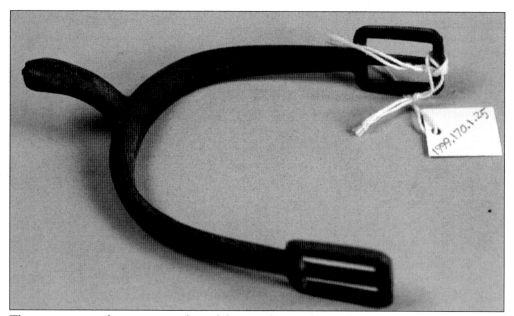

The surviving artifacts are reminders of the sacrifices and contributions made by Union men. This spur was recovered from Fort Pillow, Tennessee, and most likely belonged to a member of the 14th Tennessee Cavalry. The 14th participated in the ill-fated defense of Fort Pillow along with a regiment of U.S. Colored Artillery. The spur is a standard-issue U.S. Army enlisted spur. (TSM.)

Cavalry regiments carried small guidons such as this one. This surviving guidon belonged to an unidentified Union cavalry regiment from Tennessee. (TSM.)

In the decades after the war, veterans began to establish monuments and memorials on the battlefields on which they had fought, in their hometowns, and in the national cemeteries. This is the GAR or Union monument in the National Cemetery in Knoxville. This cemetery was established by Gen. Ambrose Burnside after the Battle of Knoxville in November 1863. (LOC.)

After the war, the federal government recovered the bodies of as many soldiers as could be found and relocated them to national cemeteries. Thousands of soldiers remained unidentified. This photograph shows the markers of the unknown Union dead buried at the Chattanooga National Cemetery. Other national cemeteries in Tennessee included Fort Donelson, Shiloh, Nashville, Memphis, Greeneville, Knoxville, and Stones River. (LOC.)

This photograph shows the surviving veterans of Company C, 1st Tennessee Cavalry. The men pose with what remains of the regimental flag. Company C was the color company of the regiment and thus had the honor of protecting the flag during the war. Although undated, this image was probably taken in the 1920s. (Knox County Two Centuries Photograph Project, McClung Historical Collection.)

After the war, the graves of Civil War casualties could be found in small cemeteries across Tennessee. This 1937 photograph shows Civil War graves near Caldwell Fork in the Great Smoky Mountains. As the last veterans died, the service of these Union men was, unfortunately, often forgotten. (Great Smoky Mountains National Park.)

BIBLIOGRAPHY

Carter, W. R. *History of the First Regiment of Tennessee Volunteer Cavalry.* Johnson City, TN: Overmountain Press, 1992.

Civil War Centennial Commission of Tennessee. *Tennesseans in the Civil War: A Military History of Confederate and Union Units with Available Rosters of Personnel.* Nashville, TN: Civil War Centennial Commission, 1965.

Current, Richard Nelson. *Lincoln's Loyalists: Union Soldiers from the Confederacy.* Boston, MA: Northeastern University Press, 1992.

Ellis, Daniel. *Thrilling Adventures of Daniel Ellis, the Great Union Guide of East Tennessee.* New York: Harper and Brothers, 1867.

Fisher, Noel. *The Civil War in the Smokies.* Gatlinburg, TN: Great Smoky Mountains Association, 2005.

Government Printing Office. *Biographical Directory of the American Congress, 1774–1927.* Washington, D.C.: Government Printing Office, 1928.

McBride, Robert M., and Dan M. Robison. *Biographical Directory of the Tennessee General Assembly, Volumes I and II.* Nashville, TN: Tennessee State Library and Archives and the Tennessee Historical Commission, 1979.

McCaslin, Richard B. *Portraits of Conflict: A Photographic History of Tennessee in the Civil War.* Fayetteville, AK: University of Arkansas Press, 2007.

McTeer, Major William A. *Among Loyal Mountaineers: The Reminiscences of a Blount County Unionist.* Maryville, TN: '27/'37 Publishing, 2007.

National Archives. *Compiled Service Records of Volunteer Union Soldiers Who Served in Organizations from the State of Tennessee, M395, Rolls 1 thru 109.* Washington, D.C.: National Archives and Records Administration.

Potter, Jerry O. *The Sultana Tragedy: America's Greatest Maritime Disaster.* Gretna, LA: Pelican Publishing, 1992.

Scott, Samuel W., and Samuel P. Angel. *History of the Thirteenth Regiment Tennessee Volunteer Cavalry, U.S.A.* Philadelphia, PA: P. W. Ziegler and Company, 1903; reprinted Johnson City, TN: Overmountain Press, 1987.

Severance, Ben H. *Tennessee's Radical Army: The State Guard and Its Role in Reconstruction, 1867–1869.* Knoxville, TN: University of Tennessee Press, 2005.

Starr, Stephen Z. *The Union Cavalry in the Civil War, Volume III: The War in the West.* Baton Rouge, LA: Louisiana State University Press, 1985.

Warner, Ezra J. *Generals in Blue: Lives of the Union Commanders.* Baton Rouge, LA: Louisiana State University Press, 1992.

Wright, Gen. Marcus J. (compiler). *Tennessee in the Civil War 1861–1865.* New York: Ambrose Lee Publishing Company, 1908; reprinted Salem, MA: Higginson Book Company.

ACROSS AMERICA, PEOPLE ARE DISCOVERING SOMETHING WONDERFUL. *THEIR HERITAGE.*

Arcadia Publishing is the leading local history publisher in the United States. With more than 4,000 titles in print and hundreds of new titles released every year, Arcadia has extensive specialized experience chronicling the history of communities and celebrating America's hidden stories, bringing to life the people, places, and events from the past. To discover the history of other communities across the nation, please visit:

www.arcadiapublishing.com

Customized search tools allow you to find regional history books about the town where you grew up, the cities where your friends and family live, the town where your parents met, or even that retirement spot you've been dreaming about.

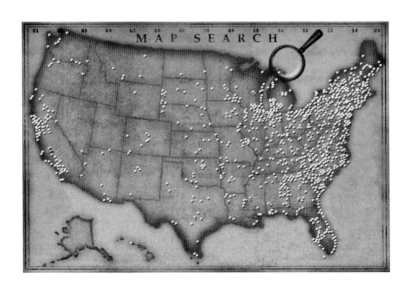